Why Did the Whole World Stop?

Talking with kids about COVID-19

Heather Black

Dedicated to the healthcare workers of the world, who spend their time caring for others every day.

ISBN: 978-1-08787-902-4

Note to Parents and Caregivers:

This book is intended to be read with your child, to help them process some of the many changes that came in response to the COVID-19 pandemic. I tried to address the topic with sensitivity and clarity, but you know your child best. Reassurance from you is the most effective comfort.

You can read an article I wrote about this here:
<u>Top 10 Tips for Talking Through Tough Topics With Kids</u>
https://themindfulmoments.com/top-10-tips-for-talking-through-tough-topics-with-kids/

It's amazing how fast the world changed in response to COVID-19.

You might be wondering:

Why is this such a big deal?

What happened?

When will things get back to normal?

Should I be scared?

When can I see my friends?

What can I do to help?

You might not even be sure what everyone is talking about!

Learning more about COVID-19 can be useful.

Coronavirus PROTECTION

This book can help you understand more about COVID-19, and even give you some ideas of how to use this unusual time for good things.

How did the novel coronavirus, COVID-19, get its name?

- <u>Novel</u>: New
- <u>Coronavirus</u>: A specific group of virus germs.
- <u>CO</u>: Corona, which means crown, because the virus looks a little like a crown under a microscope.
- <u>VI</u>: Virus, a tiny particle that only multiplies inside a living host, like a person, animal, or plant.
- <u>D</u>: Disease, something that makes people or animals sick.
- <u>19</u>: Named for the year 2019. This strain of coronavirus in people was first reported to the World Health Organization on December 31, 2019.

Who decided we should stay home?

When something major happens in the world, like a new disease that is contagious, leaders of countries and scientists work together to figure out the best way to protect people. Many things changed quickly in response to the outbreak of COVID-19.

Schools closed.

Teachers and students had to find new ways to keep learning, like online classes and homework assignments.

Playgrounds closed.

Germs can stay active for a while on surfaces, like a ladder or swing. Later, they might pass to a new person who touches that object. So, many public areas were off limits.

Events were cancelled.

Any activity that required people to get together
had to be delayed or cancelled.

Restaurants delivered food at the door or to homes.

Some businesses had to close temporarily.

Some people worked from home.

Their jobs might be done on computer or phone.

Some people were out of work.

Their jobs could only be done in contact with other people.

Some people had to go to work even more than usual.

Especially those who worked in healthcare, like doctors and nurses, might be busier than normal.

So many things changed at once, it was a little bit confusing.

People wore face masks and gloves when going out to be extra careful about germs.

Some people worried they might run out of things they needed, so they bought extra.

Shops ran out of things like toilet paper, hand sanitizer, bread, milk, and rice.

People ordered things online they might usually get from a local store.

This let them get things they needed without going out.

In some places, the government leaders told people they must be home by a certain time of night.

That's called a curfew.

Part of a police officer's job included making sure people had an important reason to be out.

Otherwise, they weren't supposed to leave their homes.

Nearly everyone around the world tried to practice social distancing.

That's staying out of large groups, keeping space between yourself and others, or simply staying home.

How does social distancing help prevent the spread of COVID-19?

- Virus germs can't move by themselves. So with fewer people going out, there are less chances for germs to spread.
- If someone gets sick, it is easier to figure out where they might have caught the virus.
- It helps keep hospitals from having too many patients at once. That allows them to serve everyone better, including those who are sick with other things, hurt, or having babies.

How Contagious is COVID-19?

Just one sneeze can spread over 20,000 droplets containing virus particles! That's why it's important to cover your face when you sneeze or cough.

What is a pandemic?

<u>Pan</u>: All   <u>Demic</u>: People

- A pandemic is when many people in different parts of the world catch the same disease at the same time.
- The World Health Organization declared COVID-19 a pandemic on March 11, 2020

COVID-19 was first discovered in the city of Wuhan, China, in December 2019. That may be far away from where you live. But many people travel to different parts of the world every day. In just a few weeks, there were outbreaks of the disease in nearly every country worldwide.

How is COVID-19 different from other diseases?

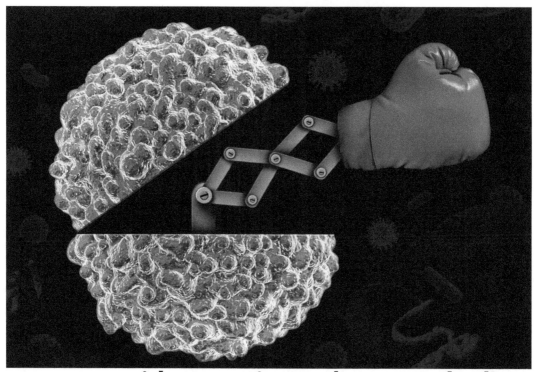

Everyone gets sick sometimes, but our bodies have immune systems to help fight disease.

Think of your immune system like a guard, and the billions of virus and bacteria particles around us like tiny travelers who want to come into your body. Bacteria and virus particles travel in and out of our bodies every single day.

Why is it spreading fast?

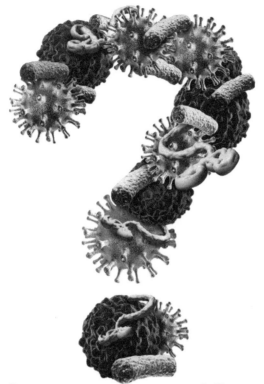

Some bacteria and viruses are good for us, or at least not very harmful, and our immune system lets them in. It quickly attacks ones that it knows might make us sick. Because the COVID-19 virus hasn't made people sick before now, our immune system doesn't know whether the virus is good or bad, so it doesn't fight it right away. We have no immunity toward COVID-19.

Is it possible to slow the spread?

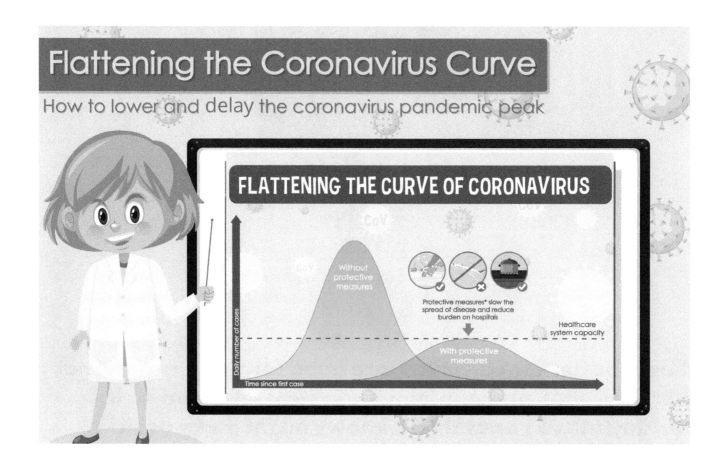

Yes! You have probably heard people talk about "flattening the curve." That means trying to reduce the number of people who get the disease at once.

Is there treatment for COVID-19?

Researchers are working hard to make specific treatments and vaccines, to fight the disease. Vaccines work by helping our immune system identify a disease, so it knows to attack those germs.

What happens if you get COVID-19?

Most people who catch COVID-19 don't get very sick. They might feel bad with a fever and cough for a little while, but their immune system is able to fight against the disease and win. They get better.
A few people can have COVID-19, but not feel sick at all, even though they are still contagious.

Hospitals can help.

For some people, the COVID-19 disease becomes more serious, and they have a hard time breathing. These people may need help with a respirator in the hospital while their immune system fights the disease.

Some pass away.

Sadly, a few people are not able to recover from the disease, and they die. This is true of many other diseases, too. But, since COVID-19 is new and widespread, it is getting lots of attention in news around the world.

You might be wondering: Is there anything I can do to help?

The answer is: Yes!

Respect social distancing guidelines.

This helps protect everyone.

Wash your hands.

1 WATER AND SOAP

2 PALM TO PALM

3 BETWEEN FINGERS

4 FOCUS ON THUMBS

5 BACK OF HANDS

6 FOCUS ON WHISTS

Clean hands help keep you healthy.

Pray for those who are sick.

Ask that they will recover soon, and that the virus spread will end.

Call someone who might be lonely.

It's great to let people know you care about them.

Get some exercise.

It's important to stay active.

Use your creativity.

Make something new with your talents.

Keep on learning.

It's always a great time to learn something new.

Help out in your home.

Do your part to keep things pleasant around the house.

Spend time with your family.

Make some great memories.

Look forward to the days when we can all get together again.

Everyday things will feel exciting and new!

Resources

What is a Virus? *Live Science* website https://www.livescience.com/53272-what-is-a-virus.html

How Vaccines Work Public Health website https://www.publichealth.org/public-awareness/understanding-vaccines/vaccines-work/

World Health Organization https://www.who.int/about

About the Author

I'm Heather Black, follower of Jesus, wife to my awesome husband, Christopher, and mom to 11 (that's not a typo... eleven!) wonderful children, ranging in age from their early 20s, down to a baby.

My family lives in New England, where we laugh often, bicker sometimes, make memories, and generally love life in a big family.

Visit my site at The Mindful Moments for some easy, fun resources to make your own family memories! https://themindfulmoments.ck.page/06b1e2678f